THE STORY OF THE
ORLANDO
MAGIC

CREATIVE ❦ EDUCATION

Published by Creative Education
123 South Broad Street
Mankato, Minnesota 56001
Creative Education is an imprint of The Creative Company.

DESIGN AND PRODUCTION BY **EVANSDAY DESIGN**

PHOTOGRAPHS BY Getty Images (Nathaniel S. Butler / NBAE, Paul
Chapman, Brian Cleary, Scott Cunningham / NBAE, Tim de Frisco
/ Allsport, Gary Dineen / NBAE, Garrett W. Ellwood / NBAE, Andy
Lyons / Allsport, Fernando Medina / NBAE, Doug Pensinger
/ Allsport, Jeff Reinking / NBAE, Terrence Vaccaro / NBAE),
SportsChrome (Brian Drake)

LIBRARY OF CONGRESS CATALOGING-IN-PUBLICATION DATA

Gilbert, Sara.
The story of the Orlando Magic / by Sara Gilbert.
p. cm. — (The NBA—a history of hoops)
Includes index.
ISBN-13: 978-1-58341-419-4
1. Orlando Magic (Basketball team)—History—
Juvenile literature. I. Title. II. Series.

GV885.52.O75G55 2006
796.323'64'0975924—dc22   2005051771

First edition

9 8 7 6 5 4 3 2 1

COVER PHOTO: *Dwight Howard*

THE STORY OF THE
ORLANDO

MAGIC

SARA GILBERT

CREATIVE ✿ EDUCATION

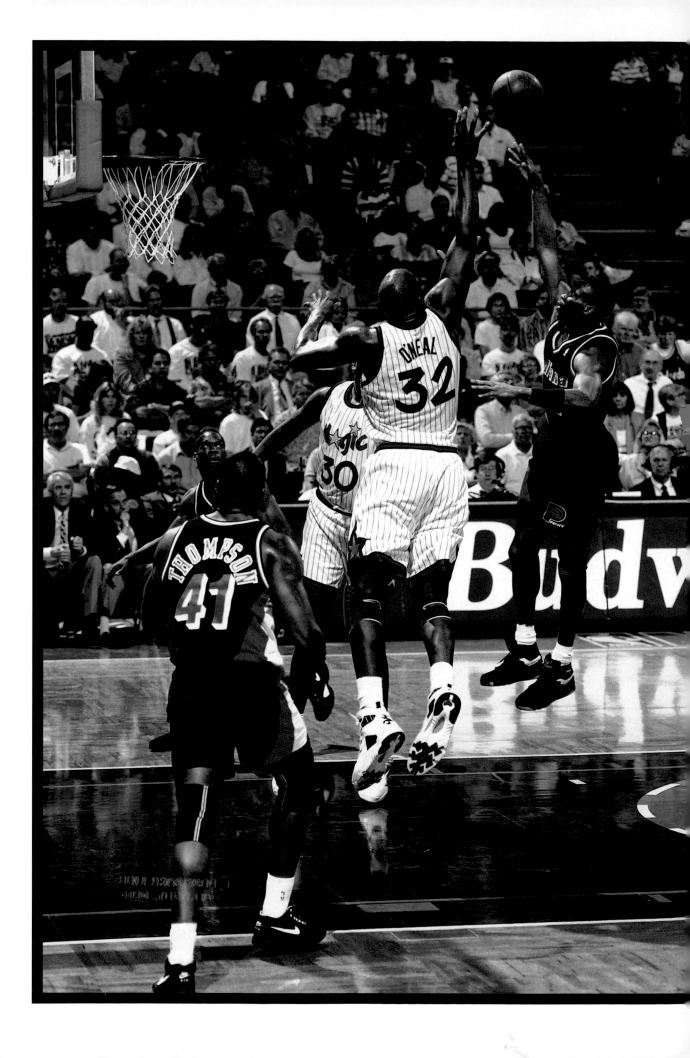

SHAQUILLE O'NEAL STEPPED ONTO THE FLOOR OF
THE ORLANDO ARENA IN 1992, HE WAS THE STAR
OF THE SHOW. THE BALL LOOKED LIKE AN ORANGE
IN THE 7-FOOT-1 AND 300-POUND CENTER'S GIANT
PALM AS HE BOWLED THROUGH THE OPPOSITION
FOR A DUNK. ON DEFENSE, HE SWATTED AWAY
SHOTS WITH ENOUGH FORCE TO SPILL POPCORN
IN THE STANDS. WITH SHAQ, THE ORLANDO MAGIC
SOARED ALL THE WAY TO THE NATIONAL BASKETBALL
ASSOCIATION (NBA) FINALS. O'NEAL EVENTUALLY
TOOK HIS MAGIC ELSEWHERE, BUT HE WILL FOREVER
BE A TOWERING FIGURE IN FRANCHISE HISTORY.

MAKING THE MAGIC

ORLANDO, FLORIDA, WAS NAMED IN HONOR OF

Orlando Reeves, a soldier who was killed during the

Seminole Wars of the 1850s. The community's warm

weather and proximity to some of the world's most

beautiful beaches have made it one of the most popular

vacation destinations in the United States.

9

Despite standing only 6-foot-1, point guard Scott Skiles was a big figure in the early years of the Magic

10

Dennis Scott hit more three-pointers (981) during his Magic career than any other player in club history

Perhaps Orlando's biggest attraction is the famous Walt Disney World amusement complex. Millions of visitors make their way to the theme parks, including Epcot Center and the Magic Kingdom. Orlando is also home to another kind of Magic—the Orlando Magic basketball team, which has been entertaining fans since joining the NBA in 1989.

Orlando's first roster was built primarily through an Expansion Draft that provided the Magic with guard Reggie Theus, forward Terry Catledge, and point guard Scott Skiles. The team also selected versatile University of Illinois swingman Nick Anderson in the 1989 NBA Draft. The Magic went 7–7 in their first month, but the rest of the season was a struggle, and the team finished at 18–64.

In 1990, Orlando drafted Georgia Tech forward Dennis Scott, who provided a much-needed offensive boost. Orlando also received inspired play from the scrappy Skiles, who set an NBA record during a 1990 game with 30 assists. Behind these players, the Magic improved to 31–51. Although injuries led to a 21–61 drop-off the next year, the Magic's poor record put them in position to make a move that would change the future of the franchise.

THE FIRST CHOICE

With the first NBA Draft pick in franchise history, the Orlando Magic selected 6-foot-6 swingman Nick Anderson from the University of Illinois. Anderson, who had averaged 18 points and almost 8 rebounds a game during his final collegiate season, would be one of Orlando's building blocks. "He can score, he can rebound, and he can play two positions," said Magic coach Matt Guokas. "He'll do a lot of learning this year, but I wish I had his future." Anderson holds the team record for career free throws made (1,614), yet many remember the four crucial free throws he missed in the final seconds of Game 1 in the 1995 NBA Finals, which helped enable the Houston Rockets to win the game and, eventually, the series.

THE O'NEAL ERA

IN 1992, THE MAGIC HAD THE TOP OVERALL PICK IN

the NBA Draft. With it, the team selected 7-foot-1 and

300-pound Louisiana State University center Shaquille

O'Neal, whose rare combination of size and strength

had scouts predicting instant stardom. In his first year,

O'Neal averaged 23 points, 13 rebounds, and almost 4

blocked shots a game, and was voted the NBA Rookie

of the Year. The young giant also led the Magic to an

improved 41–41 mark.

Probably the most powerful player in NBA history, Shaquille O'Neal turned Orlando into a contender

Then, with the first pick of the 1993 NBA Draft, Orlando chose forward Chris Webber and traded his rights to the Golden State Warriors for the rights to Memphis State University guard Anfernee "Penny" Hardaway and three future first-round draft picks. At 6-foot-7, Hardaway was taller than most point guards, yet he had the quickness and ball-handling ability to easily drive to the basket. With Hardaway and O'Neal, the Magic suddenly had one of the league's most potent duos. "I'm glad I'm getting out of this game soon," said Los Angeles Lakers forward James Worthy. "I don't want to be around when those two grow up."

When Michael Jordan unexpectedly retired in 1993 after leading the Chicago Bulls to three consecutive NBA championships, the Eastern Conference was suddenly wide open, and the Magic were ready to take their shot. In 1993–94, O'Neal and Hardaway led Orlando to a 50–32 record. Although the Magic were swept in the playoffs by the Indiana Pacers, notice had been served that Orlando was a team on the rise.

BREAKING BACKBOARDS

In his first year in the NBA, Shaquille O'Neal destroyed two backboards. On February 7, 1993, Shaq slammed a ferocious dunk at America West Arena in Phoenix, then hung on the rim, pulling the backboard forward. The back end of the base lifted off the ground, and the collapsible basket folded into its storage position, delaying the game for 35 minutes. Two months later, another powerful dunk in New Jersey ripped apart the backboard's support braces; the backboard, stanchion, and base all had to be replaced, delaying the game for more than 45 minutes. "I just went up and dunked and it broke," O'Neal said afterwards. "It really came crashing down. The shot clock hit me in the head. It hurt a little bit, but not that much. I have a hard head."

One of the biggest reasons for the Magic's quick postseason knockout was the lack of a strong forward. Before the start of the next season, Orlando added 6-foot-10 forward Horace Grant, who had won three NBA titles with the Bulls. The loaded 1994–95 Magic finished with a conference-best 57–25 mark. In the playoffs, they powered past the Bulls and all the way to the NBA Finals, where they faced the defending champion Houston Rockets. O'Neal and Hardaway each scored 26 points in Game 1, but the Rockets pulled out a 120–118 overtime victory. The loss seemed to deflate the Magic, who lost the next three games and the series. "It's a hard loss to take," O'Neal said after the series. "I thought this was our year."

The Magic returned with a vengeance in 1995–96, determined to prove that their march to the Finals was no fluke. Orlando started 17–5, driven largely by the long-range gunning of Dennis Scott, who set an NBA record with 267 three-pointers during the season. Orlando finished 60–22 and met the Chicago Bulls in the Eastern Conference Finals. But Michael Jordan had returned to Chicago, and his Bulls swept Orlando in four games.

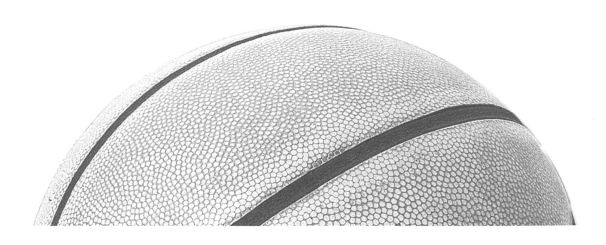

Although he rarely made headlines, Horace Grant was a valuable rebounder and stout low-post defender

HANDOFF TO HARDAWAY

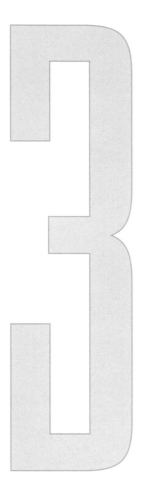

ORLANDO FANS WERE LEFT STUNNED WHEN O'NEAL departed in the off-season to chase more money and stardom with the Los Angeles Lakers. The team's fate now rested squarely on Hardaway's shoulders. "It's Penny's team now," said Horace Grant, "and we'll go as far as he takes us."

Orlando acquired veteran center Rony Seikaly to help replace O'Neal, but after a knee injury sidelined Hardaway, the team stumbled. With Orlando at 24–25, coach Brian Hill was fired and replaced by assistant Richie Adubato. The team went 21–12 the rest of the season and made the playoffs again. In the first round, the Miami Heat easily beat the Magic in the first two games. A returned Hardaway then fired back, pouring in 42 and 41 points to lead his team to victory in the next two games. In Game 5, however, the Heat held on for a 91–83 victory.

Perry Safely netted an average of 16 points per game over the course of his two-season Orlando career

8c Outlaw frequently made the evening highlights with his flair for dunking and swatting away shots.

Before the start of the next season, Chuck Daly was named Orlando's new coach. Injuries to Hardaway and Anderson crippled the team in 1997–98, yet forwards Derek Strong and Charles "Bo" Outlaw and guard Darrell Armstrong still led the Magic to a respectable 41–41 mark. "I'm very proud of these guys," said Coach Daly. "They could have quit when Nick and Penny were hurt, but they gave me all they had."

Daly's second season as Orlando's coach was shortened to 50 games due to a dispute between NBA players and owners. After the season finally started, the Magic bolted to a 33–17 record, then faced the Philadelphia 76ers in the playoffs. The teams split the first two games, but star guard Allen Iverson then led the 76ers to a convincing series victory. "It's a big disappointment," Nick Anderson said. "I thought we were a better team than this." After the season, Daly retired, and Hardaway asked to be traded.

21

A LITTLE ASSISTANCE

On December 30, 1990, Magic guard Scott Skiles set an NBA single-game record that still stands. That night, Skiles recorded 30 assists—two more than the previous record set by Boston Celtics star Bob Cousy in 1959—in the Magic's 155–116 rout of the Denver Nuggets. Skiles, who was stuck on 29 through much of the fourth quarter, fed the ball to swingman Jerry Reynolds with 19.6 seconds left in the game. When Reynolds promptly sank a 20-foot jump shot, Skiles broke into a wide grin and pointed to his teammate as the crowd at the Orlando Arena loudly recognized his record. "Right now I am on top of the world," Skiles said after the game. "I am just in a state of shock." In 2003, Skiles was named head coach of the Chicago Bulls.

TIME FOR T-MAC

IN 1999, THE MAGIC HIRED FORMER NBA GUARD and television analyst Glenn "Doc" Rivers as their new coach. Rivers's low-key style proved to be the perfect tonic for the young Magic. Predicted by many experts to finish near the bottom of their division, the Magic overachieved on almost every level during the 1999–00 season. Armstrong, Outlaw, and center John Amaechi emerged as leaders on a team that finished with a 41–41 record, and Rivers was named NBA Coach of the Year.

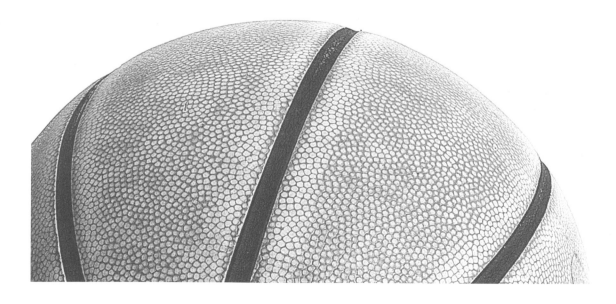

23

The normally low-key Doc Rivers led the Magic to winning records in three of his four full seasons as coach

Tracy McGrady was a scoring machine in 2002-03, pouring in an NBA-leading 32 points per game.

In 2000, the Magic made major headlines by signing both superstar forward Grant Hill and explosive swingman Tracy McGrady. "Last year we built a nucleus of guys that work hard every night and do the little things," explained Coach Rivers. "Now with the addition of Hill and McGrady, we have the weapons necessary to win the big games."

Although an injured Hill played in only four games, Rivers guided his young team to a 43–39 record in 2000–01. With McGrady averaging more than 26 points and 7 rebounds per game, the Magic made it to the playoffs for the sixth time in eight years. Magic fans were left deflated, though, as their team was quickly eliminated by the Milwaukee Bucks.

McGrady became a true NBA superstar the next season, leading the team in scoring, rebounding, and minutes played and finishing fourth in the NBA's Most Valuable Player (MVP) voting. With the help of Grant, Armstrong, and forward Mike Miller, "T-Mac" led the team to a solid 44–38 record. But once again, the Magic were defeated in the first round of the playoffs, this time by the Charlotte Hornets.

The Magic faced the same fate in 2002–03. Despite a solid showing in the regular season, the team faltered in the playoffs. Orlando took a surprising three-games-to-one series lead over the top-seeded Detroit Pistons before the Pistons fought back to win the series in seven games.

26

Formerly a star with the Detroit Pistons, Grant Hill overcame injuries to regain his form in Orlando.

AN UP-HILL BATTLE

When Grant Hill arrived in Orlando in 2000, great things were expected of the All-Star forward. But then he broke the inside bone of his left ankle and had to have season-ending surgery. Over the next three seasons, Hill played in only 43 games and underwent five more surgeries. After the fourth surgery in March 2003, he developed an infection that almost killed him. He missed all of the 2003–04 season recovering and helping his wife deal with her recently diagnosed multiple sclerosis. Few people expected to see him on the court again. But Hill returned to Orlando's lineup in 2004–05, netted almost 20 points per game, and was selected to start in the 2005 NBA All-Star Game. "It's a great story," Magic coach Johnny Davis said. "And it couldn't happen to a better person."

NEW MAGIC

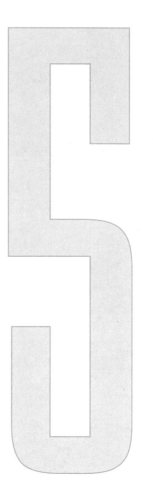

IN 2003–04, THE MAGIC LOST 19 STRAIGHT GAMES on their way to a disappointing 21–61 record. Frustrated by the losing, Tracy McGrady asked to be traded. He was soon sent (along with forward Juwan Howard) to the Houston Rockets for guard Steve Francis, and Coach Rivers was fired.

With his flashy moves and cocky attitude, Steve Francis seemed to play bigger than his 6-foot-3 size.

Boasting a rare combination of speed and power, Dwight Howard was expected to develop into a star.

MAGIC

12

RES   AND CASI

The quick and confident Francis led the 2004–05 Magic with more than 21 points per game, followed by Hill, who finally was in top form after a long series of injuries. Rookie Dwight Howard also blossomed into a standout, leading the team with 10 rebounds per game. Still, the Magic finished 36–46 and out of the playoff picture.

With their top pick in the 2005 NBA Draft, the Magic selected Fran Vazquez, a 6-foot-10 forward from Spain who they hoped would become their next star. The team also brought in as coach Brian Hill, who had led the Magic to three 50-plus-win seasons in the 1990s. "He brings a great deal of energy to the post," said Magic team president Bob Vander Weide. "The bottom line: The organization is excited to have him back, and it just feels right."

For 15-plus years, the Orlando Magic have been the model for building a successful team from the ground up. Through good times and bad, Orlando's fans have passionately supported the franchise. With the new roster of talented players rising up in central Florida, opponents may need a bit of magic themselves to stop Orlando in the seasons ahead.

IT'S ALL IN THE SHOES

When a game between the Orlando Magic and the Washington Wizards ended on December 30, 2002, Wizards guard Michael Jordan took off his gray and white Nike basketball shoes and presented them to Magic guard Tracy McGrady with this inscription: *Enjoyed the challenge. Good luck and stay healthy. Michael Jordan.* McGrady, who scored 32 points in Orlando's 112–95 drubbing of the Wizards, proudly cradled the shoes in his arms as he left the arena. "I might look at these shoes every day before I go out of the house," he said. On the brink of retirement, the 39-year-old Jordan wanted to encourage the 23-year-old McGrady with the gift. "He's getting better and better," the legendary Jordan said. "And he will get even better because he's at such a young age."

INDEX